D0202136

Duende

Winner of the 2006 James Laughlin Award of the Academy of American Poets

The James Laughlin Award is given to commend and support a poet's second book. It is the only second-book award for poetry in the United States. Offered since 1954, the award was endowed in 1995 by a gift to the Academy from the Drue Heinz Trust. It is named for the poet and publisher James Laughlin, who founded New Directions Publishing Corp.

Judges for 2006
Elizabeth Alexander
Kimiko Hahn
Terrance Hayes

Also by Tracy K. Smith

The Body's Question

Duende

POEMS BY

Tracy K. Smith

Graywolf Press

SAINT PAUL, MINNESOTA

Publication of this volume is made possible in part by a grant provided by the Minnesota State Arts Board, through an appropriation by the Minnesota State Legislature; a grant from the Wells Fargo Foundation Minnesota; and a grant from the National Endowment for the Arts, which believes that a great nation deserves great art. Significant support has also been provided by the Bush Foundation; Target; the McKnight Foundation; and other generous contributions from foundations, corporations, and individuals. To these organizations and individuals we offer our heartfelt thanks.

NATIONAL ENDOWMENT FOR THE ARTS

MINNESOTA STATE ARTS BOARD

TARGET.

Supported by the Jerome Foundation in celebration of the Jerome Hill Centennial and in recognition of the valuable cultural contributions of artists to society

This book is made possible through a partnership with the College of Saint Benedict, and honors the legacy of S. Mariella Gable, a distinguished teacher at the College. Support has been provided by the Lee and Rose Warner Foundation and the Dewitt and Caroline Van Evera Foundation.

Published by Graywolf Press
2402 University Avenue, Suite 203
Saint Paul, Minnesota 55114
All rights reserved.

www.graywolfpress.org

Published in the United States of America

ISBN 978-1-55597-475-6

2 4 6 8 9 7 5 3 1
First Graywolf Printing, 2007

Library of Congress Control Number: 2006938264

Cover design: Christa Schoenbrodt, Studio Haus

Cover photograph: Michael Kamber, "Afghanistan, 2001"

Acknowledgments

Grateful acknowledgment is made to the editors of the following journals, anthologies and websites, where versions of these poems first appeared:

Bat City Review: "When Zappa Crashes My Family Reunion"

Brick: "The Searchers," "Slow Burn"

Callaloo: "Astral," "Flores Woman," "History," "Minister of Saudade," "The Nobodies"

Gulf Coast: "Duende," "One Man at a Time," "The Opposite of War"

McSweeney's: "Astral," "Duende"

The Nebraska Review: "Theft"

Ontario Review: "Interrogative," "El Mar"

Quarterly West: "Nocturne: Andalusian Dog"

Redivider: "Western Fragment"

West Branch: "Igor at Gunpoint"

"Duende" also appears on the Academy of American Poets website (www.poets.org), *From the Fishouse* (www.fishousepoems.org), and in the anthologies *Gathering Ground: A Reader Celebrating Cave Canem's First Decade* (University of Michigan Press, 2006) and *Legitimate Dangers: American Poets of the New Century* (Sarabande, 2006).

"History" also appears in *Legitimate Dangers: American Poets of the New Century* (Sarabande, 2006), and in an anthology of visiting writers published by the Downtown Writer's Center of the YMCA of Greater Syracuse.

"The Nobodies" also appears on *From the Fishouse* (www.fishousepoems.org).

I wish to thank the Rona Jaffe Foundation, the Ludwig Vogelstein Foundation, and the Mrs. Giles Whiting Foundation for generous awards that facilitated the completion of this book. I am also grateful to the Fundación Valparaíso in Mojácar, Almería, Spain, where the kernel for this book began to germinate.

for Jean
and for my father

Contents

The *duende* does not come at all unless he sees that death is possible. The *duende* must know beforehand that he can serenade death's house and rock those branches we all wear, branches that do not have, will never have, any consolation.

FEDERICO GARCÍA LORCA
Play and Theory of the Duende

Duende

I.

History

Prologue

This is a poem about the itch
That stirs a nation at night.

This is a poem about all we'll do
Not to scratch—

Where fatigue is great, the mind
Will invent entire stories to protect sleep.

Dark stories. Deep fright.
Syntax of nonsense.

Our prone shape has slept a long time.
Our night, many nights.

This is a story in the poem's own voice.
This is epic.

⟺

Part One: Gods and Monsters

The Eagle dreams light,
Dreams molten heat, dreams words

Like *bark, fir* and great mountains
Appear under the shadows of great trees.

The Eagle dreams *fox*, and that amber shape
Appears in a glade. Dreams *egg*,

And the fox is cradling
A fragile world between sharp teeth.

All gods do this.
Flesh is the first literature.

There is Pan Gu. Dog-god.
His only verb: to grow.

And when he dies, history happens.
His body becomes Word:

Blood, eye, tendon, teeth
Become river, moon, path, ore.

Marrow becomes jade. Sperm, pearl.
The vermin of his body: you and me.

Elsewhere and at the same time,
Some sentient scrap of first flame,

Of being ablaze, rages on,
Hissing air, coughing still more air,

Sighing rough sighs around the ideas
Of *man, woman, snake, fruit.*

We all know the story
Of that god. Written in smoke

And set down atop other stories.
(How many others? Countless others.)

There is the element of Earth to consider:
Fast globe driven by the children of gods.

Driven blind, driven with fatigue, fear,
With night sweats and hoarse laughter.

Driven forward, stalled, dragged back.
Driven mad, because the ones

Who drive it are not gods themselves.

Part Two: The New World

There were always these fingers
Winding cotton and wool—
Momentary clouds—into thread.

Was always that diminishing. Words
Whittled and stretched into meaning.
And meaning here is: line.

What the fish tugs at. What is crossed.
Thin split between Ever and After.
And what, in going, is lost.

Was always the language of pigment:
Indigo, yolk, dirt red. This meant
Belonging. What the women wove:

Stark wonder. Hours and hours.
Mystery. Misery. On their knees.
A remedy for cold.

There were houses not meant to stand
Forever. But not for the reasons
We were told.

⊷

Part Three: Occupation

Every poem is the story of itself.
Pure conflict. Its own undoing.
Breeze of dreams, then certain death.

This poem is Creole. *Kreyol.*
This poem is a boat. *Bato.*
This poem floats on the horizon
All day, all night. Has leaks
And a hundred bodies at prayer.
This poem is not going to make it.

And this poem is the army
left behind when the *bato*
Sails. This poem is full
Of soldiers. *Soldas.*
When the *bato* is turned back,
The people it carries,
Those who survive, will be
Made to wish for death.
The *soldas* know how to do this.
How to make a person
Wish for death. The *soldas*
Know how to do this
Because many of them believe
They have already died once before.

There are secret police
Who don't want the poem to continue,
But they're not sure
It is important enough to silence.
They go home to wives
Who expect to be taken out,
Made love to, offered
Expensive gifts. They are bored,
The police and their wives.
They eat, turn on the TV, swallow
Scotch, wine. In bed, they say nothing,
Feigning sleep. And the house,
A new house, croons to itself.
Its voice seeps out and off,

Marries with the neighbors',
Makes a kind of American music
That holds everything in place.

Of course there are victims in this poem:

victim victim victim victim victim
victim victim victim victim victim
victim victim victim victim victim
victim victim victim victim victim
victim victim victim victim victim
victim victim victim victim victim
victim victim victim victim victim
victim victim victim victim victim
victim *you are here* victim victim
victim victim victim victim victim
victim victim victim victim victim

⊢——⊣

Part Four: Grammar

There is a *We* in this poem
To which everyone belongs.

As in: *We the People*—
In order to form a more perfect Union—

And: *We were objects of much curiosity*
To the Indians—

And: *The next we present before you*
Are things very appalling—

And: *We find we are living, suffering, loving,*
Dying a story. We had not known otherwise—

We's a huckster, trickster, has pluck.
We will draw you in.

      Your starched shirt is wet under the arms.
      Your neck spills over the collar, tie points—

      Repentant tongue—toward your bored sex.
      There is a map on the wall. A trail

      Of colored tacks spreads like a wound
      From the center, and you realize (for the first time?)

      The world is mostly water. You are not paid
      To imagine a time before tanks and submarines,

      But for a moment you do. It's a quiet thought,
      And a cool breeze blows through it. Green leaves

      Rustle overhead. Your toes sink into dark soil.

Or:

You unwrap foil from around last night's rack of lamb.
It sits like a mountain of light next to the sink.
Something inside you wants out. You calculate
Minutes and seconds on smooth keys.
There is humming, and a beeping when the food is hot.
Above your head, a bulb hangs upside down
Like an idea in reverse, tungsten filament
Sagging between prongs. Your heart sways
Like a tattered flag from the bones in your chest.
You don't think of Eisenhower, long dead,
His voice flapping away on a scrap of newsreel
From decades ago. But the silence around you
Knows he was right:

> *You have a row of dominoes set up,*
> *You knock over the first one,*
> *And what will happen to the last one*
> *Is the certainty that it will go over*
>   *very quickly.*

Or:

You settle into the plush seat
And the darkness swells, the screen
No longer silent, white. Outside
No longer today, no longer now.
Place names and years appear,

disappear like forbidden thoughts.
Chile. Cambodia. Kent State.

Why do they watch back coolly?
Why, when the lights come up,
Does a new part of you ache?
Was that you this whole time,
Running, hands in the air?
You all these years, marching
Under the weight of a gun?

We has swallowed *Us* and *Them.*
You will be the next to go.

⊷—⊶

Part Five: Twentieth Century

Sometimes, this poem wants to wander

Into a department store and watch itself
Transformed in a trinity of mirrors.

Sometimes this poem wants to pop pills.

Sometimes in this poem, the stereo's blaring
While the TV's on mute.

Sometimes this poem walks the street
And doesn't give a shit.

Sometimes this poem tells itself nothing matters, -
All's a joke. *Relax*, it says, *everything's*
Taken care of.

(A poem can lie.)

⊷

Part Six: Cosmology

Once there was a great cloud
Of primeval matter. Atoms and atoms.
By believing, we made it the world.
We named the animals out of need.
Made ourselves human out of need.
There were other inventions.
Plunder and damage. Insatiable fire.

⊷

Epilogue: The Seventh Day

There are ways of naming the wound.

There are ways of entering the dream
The way a painter enters a studio:

To spill.

Flores Woman

A species of tiny human has been discovered, which lived on the remote Indonesian island of Flores just 18,000 years ago. . . . Researchers have so far unearthed remains from eight individuals who were just one [meter] tall, with grapefruit-sized skulls. These astonishing little people . . . made tools, hunted tiny elephants and lived at the same time as modern humans who were colonizing the area.

NATURE, OCTOBER 2004

Light: lifted, I stretch my brief body.
Color: blaze of day behind blank eyes.

Sound: birds stab greedy beaks
Into trunk and seed, spill husk

Onto the heap where my dreaming
And my loving live.

Every day I wake to this.

Tracks follow the heavy beasts
Back to where they huddle, herd.

Hunt: a dance against hunger.
Music: feast and fear.

This island becomes us.

Trees cap our sky. It rustles with delight
In a voice green as lust. Reptiles

Drag night from their tails,
Live by the dark. A rage of waves

Protects the horizon, which we would devour.
One day I want to dive in and drift,

Legs and arms wracked with danger.
Like a dark star. I want to last.

The Searchers

after the film by John Ford

He wants to kill her for surviving,
For the language she spits,
The way she runs, clutching
Her skirt as if life pools there.

Instead he grabs her, puts her
On his saddle, rides back
Into town where faces
She barely remembers

Smile into her fear
With questions and the wish,
The impossible wish, to forget.
What does living do to any of us?

And why do we grip it, hang on
As if it's the ribs of a horse
Past commanding? A beast
That big could wreck us easily,

Could rise up on two legs,
Or kick its back end up
And send us soaring.
We might land, any moment,

Like cheap toys. There's always
A chimney burning in the mind,

A porch where the rocker still rocks,
Though empty. Why

Do we insist our lives are ours?
Look at the frontier. It didn't resist.
Gave anyone the chance
To plant shrubs, dig wells.

Watched, not really concerned
With whether it belonged
To him or to him. Either way
The land went on living,

Dying. What else could it choose?

September

This is the only world:
Our opaque lives. Our secrets. And that's all.
A streak of orange, a cloud of smoke unfurls.

The century's in rubble, so we curl
Around pictures of ourselves, like Russian dolls
Whose bodies within bodies form a world

Free of argument, a make-shift cure
For old-fashioned post-millennial denial.
A lake of fire. A Christ in clouds unfurled.

Knowledge is regret. Regret is pure,
But sometimes what we do with it is small.
We ride the season, married to the world.

I'm the same. Another hollow girl
Whose heart's a ripe balloon, whose demons call.
I strike a match and exhale. Smoke unfurls.

Our two eyes see in plurals:
What we understand, and what will fail.
They're both the only world.
A streak of orange, a cloud of smoke unfurls.

Letter to a Photojournalist Going-In

You go to the pain. City after city. Borders
Where they peer into your eyes as if to erase you.

You go by bus or truck, days at a time, just taking it
When they throw you in a room or kick at your gut,

Taking it when a strong fist hammers person after person
A little deeper into the ground. Your camera blinks:

Soldiers smoking between rounds. Bodies
Blown open like curtains. In the neighborhoods,

Boys brandish plastic guns with TV bravado. Men
Ask you to look them in the face and say who's right.

At night you sleep, playing it all back in reverse:

The dance of wind in a valley of dirt. Rugs and tools,
All the junk that rises up, resurrected, then disappears

Into newly formed windows and walls. People
Close their mouths and run backwards out of frame.

Up late, your voice fits my ear like a secret.
But who can hear two things at once?

Errant stars flare, shatter. A whistle, then the indescribable thud
Of an era spilling its matter into the night. Who can say the word *love*

When everything—everything—pushes back with the promise
To grind itself to dust?

>   And what if there's no dignity to what we do,
None at all? If our work—what you see, what I say—is nothing

But a way to kid ourselves into thinking we might last? If trust is just
Another human trick that'll lick its lips and laugh as it backs away?

Sometimes I think you're right, wanting to lose everything and wander
Like a blind king. Wanting to squeeze a lifetime between your hands

And press it into a single flimsy frame. Will you take it to your lips
Like the body of a woman, something to love in passing,

Or set it down, free finally, empty as the camera,
Which we all know is just a hollow box, mechanized to obey?

Sometimes I want my heart to beat like yours: from the outside in,
A locket stuffed with faces that refuse to be named. For time

To land at my feet like a grenade.

II.

El Mar

There was a sea in my marriage.
And air. I sat in the middle

In a tiny house afloat
On night-colored waves,

The current rolled in
From I don't know where.

We'd bob atop, drift
Gently out.

I liked best
When there was nothing

That I could
Or could not see.

But I know
There was more.

A map drawn on a mirror.
Globe cinched in at the poles.

Marriage is a rare game,
Its only verbs: *am*

And *are*. I aged.
Sometime ago

We sailed past bottles,
The strangest signs inside:

A toy rig. A halo of tears.
Rags like trapped doves.

Why didn't we stop?
Didn't sirens sing our names

In voices that begged with promise
And pity?

Astral

My husband is far off and thinks of me
In the past tense. I wept. I was. You
Lean into the curve your wife makes sleeping.
She is in Buenos Aires, always Buenos Aires
When she sleeps, your heft a bundle she must carry
From café to café. A child or a bag of pastries.
Her jewelry glints in daylight. What if
My foot presses down onto the white blanket
Of moonlight patching your sheet?
Where am I that I am here?

In the mountains of Wyoming
A trout looks up through the roof
Water makes. Feathers, fur, a fine
Thread of invisible chord skirt
The surface, and the trout's mind
Makes the sign for fly. Who knows
How this is done? Whether the trout
Sees the flit, the flicker on water
And recalls the brief satisfaction
Of air, the knot of legs,
Wings that collapse? And so
It leaps with its whole body.
Inveterate. And your biceps
Tighten, don't they? For a moment
You become the fish—pure muscle,
Desire tethered to desire. A stone
Skipped across this same river.
You tug back, sink the hook.

When my husband sleeps,
He makes the shirred murmur
Of sea and shore at night.
He is racing toward a gold
Disc that sits at the distance
Like an enormous yolk. It drops
Quickly, and the water glows hot.
When my husband brushes
His knuckles against her thigh,
The woman beside him smiles.
They loll on the sand.
Tiny waves nip at their feet.

Sirens wail and blare in Buenos Aires
Where your wife has caused a man's
Heart to sputter and choke, her fingers
Are that delicate. Is it her you feel
Now, when I touch the lids of your
Sleeping eyes? Your face is empty,
As if there really is a soul
That roams the planet at night. Yours
Must be heavy. Why else would you look
Now like a vacant doll, like you might rise
At the slightest effort, the faintest breeze?
And distant. Farther than the river,
Than the trout now, which has left
The river forever, unless there is a river
It remembers and traces with the memory
Of its own slick shape, terse weight.

Maybe desire is nothing but memory,
And we dream only what has already been.

Your wife falls in love with a dark man
Who leads her from ballroom to ballroom.
Their love is a slow tango. They dance
Without pause, knowing that one day
A bell will wake them, that she'll weep,
And he'll recede into the traffic of Buenos Aires,
Waving with his one raised arm
Like a figurine in an aquarium. My husband
Kicks at the sand and traces the shape
Of the woman beside him. A silhouette
Against the night sky. So many stars.
Her long hair moves like reeds
In the breeze. *Soon,* she tells him,
All the sand will be rearranged.

Minister of *Saudade*

The famous saudade of the Portuguese is a vague and constant desire for something that does not and probably cannot exist, for something other than the present, a turning towards the past or towards the future; not an active discontent or poignant sadness but an indolent dreaming wistfulness.

A.F.G. BELL, *IN PORTUGAL*

1.

The water is full of blue paint
From all the little fishing boats
Corralled for Sunday, abob in the breeze.
What kind of game is the sea?

Lap and drag. Crag and gleam.
That continual work of wave
And tide, like a wet wind, blowing
The earth down to nothing.

Our lives are small. And mine
Is small and sharp. I try to toss it
Off into the distance, forget it
For good. Then my foot steps down

Onto an edge and it's mine again,
All prick and spine. Like a burr
Deep in winter fur. And I am
Most certainly that bear. Famished,

Just awake to spring, belly slack,
Eyes still weak to the light. And where's
My leash, my colored ball? Where
Are the little fish I'm to catch in the air?

The sky here is clear of cloud and bird,
Just the sun blaring steadily through ether.
What moves is invisible. Like music.
I move in it, into it. It feels

Like nothing, until it lets me go.

2.

An old woman and a boy sit in a doorway
At the top of the hill in Pelourinho. Her mouth
Chews the corner of a towel like an engine,
Churning its way toward progress. Industry.

That's one way of describing how she moves
From table to table with just her eyes, looking
From what she wants to you and back again
While the boy sleeps. His shirt asks, *Quem*

Tenh Jesus no ❤ *?* And you remember those old
Drawings of Christ with his hand raised to knock
Against a shut door, that look of transcendent patience
Bathing his face. This woman wants your beer,

And she rises to her feet to prove it. The boy's head
Rolls back against the wall and his mouth
Hangs wide, like the hinges have sprung. Life rises
And falls under his shirt. Maybe his heart is so full

It will keep him from waking before the woman's
Good and drunk. Maybe the beer goes straight in
Like a spirit, luring her mind elsewhere, free as the voices
That float above the top of Pelourinho and out to the sea.

Some of them beg without cease. Some are singing.

3.

Igor, I wake in my hotel
And hear your steps
Disappearing down the corridor.

You, rushing away again
Into some small kitchen
On the far side of the city.

There's the fan, slicing the air
And sending it back, like a letter
Long with impossible promises.

But I'm happy alone, I say to the woman
Beside me at the bar. We drink long
into the evening, taking hours

To clarify the simplest ideas.
She writes *macumba*—witchcraft—
On my napkin. Music drowns out the sea.

Deliver us from memory.

I Don't Miss It

But sometimes I forget where I am,
Imagine myself inside that life again.

Recalcitrant mornings. Sun perhaps,
Or more likely colorless light

Filtering its way through shapeless cloud.

And when I begin to believe I haven't left,
The rest comes back. Our couch. My smoke

Climbing the walls while the hours fall.
Straining against the noise of traffic, music,

Anything alive, to catch your key in the door.
And that scamper of feeling in my chest,

As if the day, the night, wherever it is
I am by then, has been only a whir

Of something other than waiting.

We hear so much about what love feels like.
Right now, today, with the rain outside,

And leaves that want as much as I do to believe
In May, in seasons that come when called,

It's impossible not to want
To walk into the next room and let you

Run your hands down the sides of my legs,
Knowing perfectly well what they know.

Igor at Gunpoint

Everything important happens at night,
Remember?

This isn't a joke.
When I say so, you're gonna raise up your hands.

For years, your back to me made a continent.
I roamed it. Like wading the desert after dark.

Nice and slow. Now higher.

                              Faraway voices
Reached me as indecipherable sound, sped past.

And when I say so, one at a time,
You're gonna empty your pockets.

You were a world, do you understand?

You—did I stutter?—

All night wind raced the plains. I lived there
Alone, not wanting to leave.

                              You. And you.

Sometimes, I want to remind you of something.

Don't fool with me. You'll get hurt.

Diego,

Winter is a boa constrictor
Contemplating a goat. Nothing moves,
Save for the river, making its way
Steadily into ice. A state of consternation.

My limbs settle into stony disuse
In this city full of streetlamps
And unimaginable sweets.
I would rather your misuse, your beard

Smelling of some other woman's
Idle afternoons. Lately, the heart of me
Has grown to resemble a cactus
Whose one flower blooms one night only

Under the whitest,
The most disdainful of moons.

Western Fragment

And I said:

We were tired of dry spells, the whole town
Knee-deep in drought. When air stirred,
Only bone responded—that empty clack
And rattle of a body hungry for some peace.

We girls took to wearing dresses. Flowered
Dresses that pointed where the wind went.
Bore witness. Sucked parsley. Stroked
Ourselves, thinking leather, like lovers

Of some drowned outlaw. We'd wake
Wishing for something slow down the throat,
Like mules hitched always to the same spot,
Hooves wearing their groove into plank.

And you said:

The crossing was too narrow.
By the time we watered the cattle
Most of them were half dead.
We were, too, but we didn't show it.
That's not what men do.

We pitched our tents, tied
The herd, ate what we could kill.
A man doesn't have time to think

About a woman when the sky's
That vast, that bright and near.

When a man's on his horse,
And the sun's behind his back,
If the cattle are contented,
Then he might think about
A woman, women.

After Persephone

At a certain point, it didn't matter.
I commanded him to lead.
Farther. So far I was no longer me
Long before I was no longer safe.

I shed everything, save being.
There is a moment, even in the face
Of defeat, when the chase alone
Is enough. I lived quickly,

My whole life disappearing
From around me like a sound
That rises into the air and is gone
Without even an echo. After song

There is a pang. The heart in clench.
Then memory. Then retreat
Into the present. That silence.
Not emptiness, but weight.

I felt my steps marking the space
Where I must tread. Then it was I
Who led. Dragging us both
Into his world. It was real. More real

Even than what came after.

To Burn with a Low Blue Flame

There is a vessel.
You ask, and I give
Myself over. I fill it,
Knowing the descent
To be what it will always
Be. Knowing my heat
Is merely pretext
For what you'll give
Yourself into
When my heat reaches you.
I am not
What you intend me to be.
I know nothing
Of what your body knows
When it seeks
To empty out of itself.
Nor what it seeks
To forget. Or to fill.

One Man at a Time

I take a man in my arms
And my eyes roll back,
Like a doll that needs
To be sat up. The world

Is dangerous. Look
What we do to one another,
As if nothing but having
Will sustain us. Not

The having, but the taking.
I want, I want. You,
Then me. The struggle
To give everything away.

Those times it's not love
That resides there, is it,
But a lunatic colt,
Hoof to plank all night

Till the door gapes wide.
As though something
Deep in us must be tapped,
Rooted out. And so we try,

Slowly at first, like prowlers,
Until we arrive at certainty,
And that part of us quickens—
In panic? In joy? We fight back,

Eyes open, but blank, blind,
Choking on it, again and again,
Until it curls back
And we believe it is gone.

It's the loneliest work there is.
We do it thinking it better
Than the loneliness even of war.
But look at the wreckage.

There was one man I couldn't resist.
He carried himself like the leader
Of a small nation whose citizens
Whispered about his extravagant wife

And brewed their own beer
In basements hung with forbidden flags.
His hands were rough. Like the hands
Of a mechanic. When they touched me

I hummed and whirred like a radio
Tuned to disaster. When he bent down
To fasten his shoes, then kissed me
Quickly on his way back up,

Clarity settled in the room like dust
Or a layer of soot.

Poem in Which Nobody Says "I Told You So"

The point is, you won't necessarily know
Whether you're living a science fiction reality.
Just as you won't learn until after the final episode
Whether the captain meant all he said about aviation
And his wife. And what were you doing, anyway,
In that chamber? Signs everywhere whispered *Caution*.
In the past, horses were the chief vehicle
Of man's dream of escape. Then the locomotive.
Now we can lose ourselves in six dimensions.
I plead the Fifth. Lust is real. Love
Is a momentary lapse of treason. Technology
Means there is no such thing as persistence
Of vision. The West was never won.
You were never the one in the many.
But oh, the many. . . .

Now That the Weather Has Turned

Ice cakes the ground. We break
Into something with every careful step.

Nothing disappears. Only hovers and thins.
Whoever we were months ago is colder.

Someone writes to say I bear down upon him
Like a wet coat. Just these lines.

Once, I wanted everything to come to me at once.
A house converged upon by headlights. A door

Muscled open by strangers, distant cousins,
Uniforms and stenciled badges.

When they came, I let them in, gesturing
Toward the comfortable chair, crisp sheets.

Now I finger the smooth objects forgotten
By I don't know whom. They tremble

Like eggs in a shallow drawer.

Duende

1.

The earth is dry and they live wanting.
Each with a small reservoir
Of furious music heavy in the throat.
They drag it out and with nails in their feet
Coax the night into being. Brief believing.
A skirt shimmering with sequins and lies.
And in this night that is not night,
Each word is a wish, each phrase
A shape their bodies ache to fill—

> *I'm going to braid my hair*
> *Braid many colors into my hair*
> *I'll put a long braid in my hair*
> *And write your name there*

They defy gravity to feel tugged back.
The clatter, the mad slap of landing.

2.

And not just them. Not just
The ramshackle family, the *tíos,*
Primitos, not just the *bailaor*
Whose heels have notched
And hammered time
So the hours flow in place
Like a tin river, marking
Only what once was.

Not just the voices scraping
Against the river, nor the hands
Nudging them farther, fingers
Like blind birds, palms empty,
Echoing. Not just the women
With sober faces and flowers
In their hair, the ones who dance
As though they're burying
Memory—one last time—
Beneath them.
         And I hate to do it here.
To set myself heavily beside them.
Not now that they've proven
The body a myth, parable
For what not even language
Moves quickly enough to name.
If I call it pain, and try to touch it
With my hands, my own life,
It lies still and the music thins,
A pulse felt for through garments.
If I lean into the desire it starts from—
If I lean unbuttoned into the blow
Of loss after loss, love tossed
Into the ecstatic void—
It carries me with it farther,
To chords that stretch and bend
Like light through colored glass.
But it races on, toward shadows
Where the world I know

And the world I fear
Threaten to meet.

3.

There is always a road,
The sea, dark hair, *dolor*.

Always a question
Bigger than itself—

> *They say you're leaving Monday*
> *Why can't you leave on Tuesday?*

III.

Slow Burn

We tend toward the danger at the center.
Soft core teeming blue with fire. We tend
Toward what will singe and flare, but coil
Back when brought near. Sometimes we read
About people pushed there and left to recover.
They don't. Come out mangled or not at all,
Minds flayed by visions no one can fathom.

I have a cousin who haunts the basement
Of my aunt's house, drinking her liquor.
The air around him is cold, and he swings at it,
Working himself into a sweat like a boxer
Or an addict. Sometimes he comes upstairs
To eat her food, feeding the thing inside him.
We laugh, thinking laughter will make us safe,

Then we go home and lie down in our lives.
Sometimes when my thoughts won't sit still,
I imagine Marcus down there awake in the dark,
Hands fisted in his lap, or upturned, open
In what might be a kind of prayer. I'm certain
The same thing dragging his heart drags ours,
Only he's not afraid to name it. Can call it up

Into the room and swear at it, or let it rest there
On the couch beside him till his head slumps
Onto his chest and the TV bruises the walls
With unearthly light.

Interrogative

1. Falmouth, Massachusetts, 1972

Oak table, knotted legs, the chirp
And scrape of tines to mouth.
Four children, four engines
Of want. That music.

What did your hand mean to smooth
Across the casket of your belly?
What echoed there, if not me—tiny body
Afloat, akimbo, awake or at rest?

Every night you fed the others
Bread leavened with the grains
Of your own want. How
Could you stand me near you,

In you, jump and kick tricking
The heart, when what you prayed for
Was my father's shadow, your name
In his dangerous script, an envelope

Smelling of gun-powder, bay rum,
Someone to wrestle, sing to, question,
Climb?

2. Interstate 101 South, California, 1981

Remember the radio, the Coca-Cola sign
Phosphorescent to the left, bridge
After bridge, as though our lives were
Engineered simply to go? And so we went

Into those few quiet hours
Alone together in the dark, my arm
On the rest beside yours, our lights
Pricking at fog, tugging us patiently

Forward like a needle through gauze.
Night held us like a house.
Sometimes an old song
Would fill the car like a ghost.

3. Leroy, Alabama, 2005

There's still a pond behind your mother's old house,
Still a stable with horses, a tractor rusted and stuck
Like a trophy in mud. And the red house you might
Have thrown stones at still stands on stilts up the dirt road.

A girl from the next town over rides in to lend us
Her colt, cries when one of us kicks it with spurs.
Her father wants to buy her a trailer, let her try her luck
In the shows. They stay for dinner under the tent

Your brother put up for the Fourth. Firebugs flare
And vanish. I am trying to let go of something.
My heart cluttered with names that mean nothing.
Our racket races out to the darkest part of the night.

The woods catch it and send it back.

4. But let's say you're alive again—

Your hands are long and tell your age.
You hold them there, twirling a bent straw,
And my reflection watches, hollow-faced,
Not trying to hide. The waiters make it seem

Like Cairo. Back and forth shouting
That sharp language. And for the first time
I tell you everything. No shame
In my secrets, shoddy as laundry.

I have praised your God
For the blessing of the body, snuck
From pleasure to pleasure, lying for it,
Holding it like a coin or a key in my fist.

I know now you've known all along.

I won't change. I want to give
Everything away. To wander forever.
Here is a pot of tea. Let's share it
Slowly, like sisters.

When Zappa Crashes My Family Reunion

My eight aunts titter. *Look at all that hair.* He takes a plate
And a seat near Mary, whose Newport burns in a saucer
At her feet. When Zappa speaks, his magnificent nose
Reverberates like a canyon where the bear has just yawned.

Great googely moogely! Mary ashes her skirt. Gert,
On my father's side, smoothes her blouse, electric with static.
Zappa slides a long foot toward the amp, sweeps guitar to hip,
Rakes the strings like an epileptic till the goblets topple and burst.

My aunts keep their knees clasped tight, as if a piece of ice,
Or a marble that burns, might shake loose between their thighs.
Speakers fart and chirp. Somewhere in the vast Los Angeles
Of his mind, a thimbleful of plasticized dust bursts

Into purple flame. This is earnest. The bwap and waddle
Catches Uncle Richmond under the collar. He sweats, grins.
The sinclavier giggles. Mary's cigarette snuffs out at the filter
And her left shoe dangles like a tipped wig. She smiles

Way back to the sides of her mouth. *This fool is crazy!*
Somewhere else in the city of New Orleans, a woman watches
The panes in her windows rattle hard against wood. Then she listens:
Val-a-rie. Val-a-rie. Don't you want me? Don't you need me?

It sounds like a heartfelt kazoo. She puts her palm to the glass,
Then laughs. In the morning, she'll go out front still in her gown
And knock the little jockeys off the rich people's lawns. A house down,
A man slides his empty plate towards his wife. What he really means is:

There's something gliding slowly up our block and it sounds
Like amusement park music. Like a houseboat full of marionettes.
Makes me want to put on my gaiters and go. So—goodbye—he goes.
Which is just another way of saying: *Ain't this boogey a mess?*

Back at our semi-annual family reunion, Zappa winds all the cables
Up tight, lays his guitar like a dummy back in the casket. Nobody says,
Come again next time, Frank. We'll meet you in Cleveland. All the
    dumb dogs
Go right on braying at planes they think are stars. Aunt Neet fingers

The ring his glass has left on the table. No coaster. What she means is:
I want the kind of life people get dragged from early.

Theft

In 1963 John Dall, a Ho-Chunk Indian, was taken from his mother's home as part of a federal project to reduce poverty in Native American communities. He moved from foster home to foster home, haunted by recurring dreams and unsure of his own history. Years later, he was located by members of his tribe.

The word Ho-Chunk means "people of the big voice."

THE CHICAGO READER

The world shatters
Through Mother's black hair.
I breathe smoke,
Tincture of sudden berries.
Mother covers my eyes,
But this heat is inside.
It trickles out, a map
Of hot tears across my face.
And rivers, my own rivers,
Pushing out from the desert
Between my legs.

Frantic birds lift off
And their flight takes me.
I float above dark thickets,
Thick air. Above voices
That rush and rise. A mad cloak.
Sirens in my mother's mouth.
Sirens in the far corners
Of the flat black globe.

I wake again and again,
Ears ringing, eyes dry.

⟵

One night when our bellies groan,
I quiet myself watching bare branches
Scratch against the moon. If night
Has a voice, it is surely this wind
In these trees. Is surely Mother's
Heavy shoes climbing the steps,
Trampling leaves. I am the only one
Who knows what that voice means
To say. It is trying to tell us
To hurry. But it does not say
For what.
                    One brother twirls
A pencil over a notebook. Answers
He's erased hover like stalled ghosts.
He shakes his head. All wrong.
Another laughs at the TV. We are many,
Each in his own Now. I have never
Thought to cross from mine to theirs,
But I've held my hand inches
From my brother's back and felt
His heat.
                    A knock at the door,
The walls cough. Again.
And mother doesn't ignore it.
I feel what the moon must feel

For the branches night after night.
This can't go on. Come in.
Then I watch our house come undone
And Mother get smaller,
And the road ahead like a serpent
Racing into pitch.
                    In the station,
We get blankets and a civics lesson.
We get split up. All night
The drunks and devils
Sing, rattle.

⇌

I live:

    In the house behind the chain link fence
    With smoke stenciling the sky above the roof
    In a room with three boys
    And a window that wheezes winter

I wear my hair shorn

The mother here leans
Against the kitchen counter
Scrubbing forks and bowls
Staring into steam
If you interrupt her
She'll surprise you with an elbow
The back of her hand
Her fist squeaks in yellow gloves

I live in Chicago
In America

We have rules:
Don't flush
Unless necessary
And only four squares
Of tissue a day—
Two in the morning
Two at night or
All at once
But just four
And someone
Is counting

When you brush
Turn the water on once
Then off
Then on again
Say *Sir* and *Ma'am*
But only when necessary
Otherwise don't talk
And don't stare
What are you stupid
And what kind of Indian
Are you   What kind
If you don't know
You must not be

This is my eighth home
I am seven

⟷

When I skip school, I get on the El
And scour the city from inside,
From above. I listen to

The iron percussion, track
Soldered to track. A story
That turns and returns,

Refuses to end. I ride it,
Write it down: I'm in my seat
In the first car. A hologram

In the window, in the battered doors.
A stick figure in the chrome poles.
I reach for myself. Grab me by the neck.

What do I hear? Time.
What does it say? I can't tell.
What does it sound like? It sounds

Angry. Why angry? Because we keep it
Waiting. When it's not waiting,
It is always begging us to go.

I get off the train. Walk backwards
Over bridges. Watch perspective
Diminish. Watch my breath,

My ideas hover and drift
In perfect clouds. They'll
Drop eventually, mingle

With a river or lake. Might
Even one day make it back to me.
As rain, maybe, or a tall glass

I drink quickly, blind
With thirst. I shout my name
Into the traffic, and if my voice

Is big enough, someone will hear it.
It will land where it needs to land,
And someone will catch it

And come looking.

"I Killed You Because You Didn't Go to School and Had No Future"

*Note left beside the body of
nine-year-old Patricio Hilario,
found in a Rio street in 1989*

Your voice crashed through the alley
Like a dog with tin cans tied to its tail.

Idiot pranks. At the sight of your swagger
Old women prayed faster, whispered.

Their daughters yelled after you. Little shit.
Delinquent. You couldn't even read

What we wrote about kids like you. Today,
Heat wends up from the neighbors' houses

Like fear in reverse. Your uncle
Wears trousers and perspires

Into the seams of his shirt. His only belt
Is full of new holes and nearly circles you twice.

"Into the Moonless Night"

Kidnapped as teenagers nine years ago by the Lord's Resistance Army in Uganda, [Charlotte Awino, Grace Acan, Janet Akello and Caroline Anyango] were given as "wives" to rebel commanders and forced to bear their children.

THE NEW YORK TIMES MAGAZINE

CHORUS:

What's more important? The beginning
Or the end? That they went
Or that they returned? And what is over?
Did the pain end each time the hand
Whip stick belt was lifted?

Let us be them.

Let us be their captors. Let us be
The village they were dragged from,
The families murdered, the President
In stiff gabardine, cordoned by cameras
And glinting badges.

Let us be ourselves
Thinking other thoughts, wanting
To be loved fed touched bought
Fucked protected moved left-alone.

JENNIFER:

We were led out into the night,
Persuaded by their bright bayonets,
Dragged by our gowns,
Tied together, trampled. Led
By boys from the neighboring school
Who were no longer boys. Child soldiers,
Eyes cloudy as marbles.
They kicked at us. We marched.
Later, I fled. Hid. Was found. Other girls
Were handed sticks and made
To deliver blow after blow. Expeditious.
I died and was left in plain view, an example
To be whittled by maggots and birds.

This is not myth.
My body did not sing. It stank.

CHORUS:

Where were they?

Asleep

How did the boys come?

By storm

Was there a rape?

It lasted 8 years

CHARLOTTE:

We were just distributed like shoes.
My husband had 21 wives.

GRACE:

I was given to an old man.
He was very rude, very cruel.

JANET:

I was given to a disabled man.
He was not rude; he was nice.

CHORUS:

What about the parents?

ANGELINA:

I refused to receive my daughter
Unless all the girls were released.

I waited years and years.
My waiting was famous.

How would it look
If I loved my daughter

More than I love mankind?

CHORUS:
[singing]

Could the Lord ever leave you?
Could the Lord ever forget his love?

Though the mother forsakes her child,
He will not abandon you.

ANGELINA:

How would it look
If I loved my own daughter
More than I love mankind?

JOSEPH KONY:

I am the Chosen Son.
Eight angels abide in me,
Guide me toward peace
For this country. It will
Rain down like blood.

Lamb and lion, I am godly.
And if I fall, I will be
Resurrected. And if
I suffer wounds, I will
Lay my hand upon them
And the wounds will recede.

I am one part of three:
The Son, who is
The Father, who is
The Blessed Ghost
That imparts Glory.

I am whole in spirit.
I am holy
Through and through.

WIVES:
[56 women, in unison.]

He is like a mighty father.
He protects us
From danger, massacre.

And we are safer
When he is among us,
For he is mighty, our father.

He gives orders.
We comply out of trust.
We feared danger, massacre

When we were the daughters
Of villagers. We were mortal once.
Now we serve a mighty father
Of danger, massacre.

ALICE LAKWENA:

The Movement was the plan of the Lord
It was not my plan   I was taken ill
Go to Paraa   God told me   And I went to Paraa
Speak to the animals   And I spoke to the animals   I said
You animals   God sent me to ask whether you bear responsibility
For the bloodshed in Uganda   And they told me   *No*
The buffalo displayed a wounded leg   The hippopotamus
Displayed a wounded arm   God told me
Speak to the water   And I spoke to the water   I said
Water   I am coming to ask you about the sins
And bloodshed in this world   And the water said
Man kills his brethren and deposits the bodies in the water
God told me   *go to Mount Kilak*   And I went to Kilak
Speak to the mountain   And I spoke to the mountain   I said
God has sent me to find out why there is theft in the world
And the mountain said   *I have gone nowhere I have stolen*
Nothing   And God said there was a tribe
That was hated everywhere
                              This tribe was the Acholi

ACHOLI VILLAGERS:

They cut off noses and ears.
They will cut off your sex!

They will kidnap your children
Then send them to kill you.

They will seal your lips shut
With a stake and padlock.

You will not even be able
To scream in anguish.

They use holy oil to keep away bullets.
They use songs to slay the enemy.

Their sticks become swords.
Their rocks grenades.

JANET:

I beat a ten-year-old boy to death.
Blood came from his ears and nose.

I was ordered to beat him with a big stick.
I liked him. He looked me in the face as he died.

PRESIDENT MUSEVENI:

We have a country to run
        They have Holy Spirit mystic nonsense
We have helicopters   tanks   trucks
        They have ragtag children   guerilla girls

GRACE:

After an army attack
I found my son's shirt
And his arm in a tree.

CAROLINE:

There was a kind of comfort
In the other women.
Lost girls surviving
By the smallest acts.
The ones who lasted
Were strong. The ones
Who didn't were some
Of the best of us. Would have
Become something valuable
In another place.

JANET:

Why did I love life?
And if I loved it, why
Didn't I lose it?

CHORUS:

Now—please. Tell us:
How does it end?

GRACE:

(Does it end?)

CHARLOTTE:

Somewhere in every life there is a line.
One side to the other and you are gone.
Not disappeared, but undone.

JANET:

What time does not heal, it destroys.
I beat a rug and my own body stiffens with the memory.

GRACE:

Come. We girls are not supposed to be out after dark.

The Opposite of War

Their bodies want to love.
They sway and dart with a grace
That can only be affection.

The twitch, the flicker
Of fire under the skin. Look
At the wrist, like a bird

About to talon a squirrel.
But he will sink, swerve,
Emerge above or behind

And his opponent will return
To the simplest of dances:
Ginga. Ginga. Like water

In wind. Where does anything
Begin? Light flares and departs
The spine. Flame along a fuse.

Something reacts faster
Than language in the mind.
And something listens, lets go.

Kids holler into the circle,
Hop and shimmy along the fringe.
Two a little farther off to the side

Flip their bodies into the air,
Fearless of landing. What's heavy
Grounds us to the world.

What soars teases. Look:
Now one is inverted, legs
Aswirl. He could stay like that

Forever, kicking back logic
Like the stranger at a banquet
Who chooses two glistening pears

And walks off to eat them alone.

Costa Chica

Here, coast cleaves to hill and haggard road.

Shattered glass glints out from cement walls. Green,

A shade of gold. Ordinary bottles glare ice-white.

The grass is wild. Waist high and dry as ink, swarming

With reedy music. Wade in and daylight will rush you.

Waves of wind, voices that warn in a language

Like rumor. A sow sprawls by the side of a house.

The small pigs, botched with dirt, wriggle at her side.

A girl shakes a stick, yells insults at the shadows

In her doorway. They'll make a mess of the yard:

Eggshells, small bones to snap underfoot. Have you

Ever seen a town with no doors? An old woman

Tips a bucket over her head. Sunlight in rivulets

Chases the suds down her shoulders. Her blouse

Waits like a snake in coils, asleep. You can feed

That goat, but be careful: he'll glare at the ground,

Then spring like a jack-in-the box. Pray

The rope holds. Trash here gets burned.

Only men contemplate the sea, motor out in boats

Called *Victoria* and *Patty*, to where the giant fish sleep.

Ask and they'll take you. The liquid's a smooth blue,

Warm and deep, alive. It breathes in and you rise

To a startling height. Then it breathes out. It's funny

The little boat doesn't tip. A fish is pure muscle.

Miracle in water. The men dive down with spears,

Come up, mouths wide. There's something reckless

About these girls. They walk slow, barefoot, eating

Corn on a stick, laughing into everyone's eyes.

If there's anything you lack, ask. Anyone

Will try to help, will hold onto your question

Like a lozenge, tongue churning, tasting an answer.

In Brazil

for Adélia Prado

Poets swagger up and down the shore, I'll bet,
Wagging their hips in time to the raucous tide.
They tip back their heads and life sears a path
Down the throat. At night they dance, don't they,
Across tiles that might as well be glass, or ice.
And if they don't want to spend the evening alone,
They don't. And if they want to wear snow-angels
Into the sheets of some big empty bed, that's
What they do, until a dark form takes shape
On the ceiling overhead. Then they put on a robe
And kick around looking for some slippers.
When the poem finally arrives, it grins
And watches back with wide credulous eyes.

Vaya, Camarón

for Camarón de la Isla

You have no soul now,
But are one. Anchorless child,
Wisp of whim, of sentient wind.

And your voice, which has always
Roved the earth, always dragged
Those dirt, those cobbled roads,

Always snagged at the living like a stick
That stokes at embers and is singed—
Your voice, Ragged Traveler, hangs on

Tapping out its swift dance. Too swift
To follow with anything but abandon.

It used to be, you'd open your mouth
And the weather changed. You'd
Open your mouth and the sky'd spill

That dry, missing-somebody kind of rain
No matter the season. And it hurt
Like a guitar hurts under the right hands.

Like a good strong spell. Now
You're all song. Body gone to memory.
And guess what? It hurts

Harder.

Nocturne: Andalusian Dog

I rise. I pant. I scrape
The pavement with my
Scamper. I howl

At nothing in particular.
The moon:
Wholly empty.

My yelping pups
Are slumped now
In alleys, scorched wells.

They sleep on roofs.
Mate under quays.
Rob, rove. Pure urge.

Isn't there anything
You've lived wanting
Like a dream that won't

Resolve? No ladder.
No chest of drawers.
And so you go on

Sniffing hems, licking
At scraps, thinking
Let me rest here

On this parched mound
Of earth. On the back
Of this giant, dormant

Beast, extinct now
All but the memory
Of its one rumbling need.

As if the thought itself
Were a fistful of straw
You could drag across

Every body, every bone
And shred that pushes
Your elbows down,

Your tail up in heat.
There are men here
Who would wound me

As if I were a woman.
There are these men
Everywhere. They leap.

They kick at my ribs.
I show them my teeth.
Black flowers bloom

From their sides.
I steal. I lie
On my back in the sun,

Haul my shadow
Through traffic. I watch
For when the shepherd's

Been drinking.
I rehearse comfort:
It is brief.

If I see an egg
Or a speck of meat,
I take it. People pass

From door to door,
Seeking what may not exist.
My death will come on wheels

And leave no trail.
Like a god,
I believe in nothing.

The Nobodies

Los nadies: los hijos de nadie, los dueños de nada.
Los nadies: los ningunos, los ninguneados

EDUARDO GALEANO

1.

They rise from the dawn and dress.

They raise the bundles to their heads
And their shadows broaden—
Dark ghosts grounded to nothing.

They grin and grip their skirts.

They finger the gold and purple beads
Circling their necks, lift them
Absently to their teeth. They speak

A language of kicked stones.

And it's not the future their eyes see,
But history. It stretches
Like a dry road uphill before them.

They climb it.

2.

With small hands
They pat wet earth
Into brick.

And we wonder
What they eat
And why they believe

In their gods
With faces
Like frightening toys.

We pay what they ask,
Minus something
For our trouble,

Wondering why they don't
Pack up from the foot
Of the volcano,

Why they ruin their hands,
Their teeth, why they swallow
What they are given

Without a smile,
Or the hint of anger.

3.

A goat watches with eyes the inverse of danger,
Knowing there will always be some wafer of meaning
To savor on the tongue. Its munching
Is belief in the body and in the long dry grass.
What it finds, it takes into its mouth as proof
that necessity is the same as plenty.

The child who tends the goat
Sits on his knees in the shade of a low tree.
He considers what he knows. He lies down
On his side, takes the teat into his mouth
And drinks. What he does not know
Flickers in the breeze, brushes past his cheek,

The tip of his ear, and is quickly behind him.

4.

If it is true that the earth respires,
That it speaks only to those
Who command nothing—

If it is true that the first man
Was fashioned of corn.
Of divine shit. Of dust—

If a bale of cotton—

If color is trance,
And trance is to ride the back
Of the first great bird
In first flight—

If the world has ended twelve times—

If the atom is cognizant, coy;
If light is both pow-wow
And tango—

If, at the final trumpet,
Oil magnates will kiss the ankles
Of earth-caked girls who traipse
Along the highway's edge,
Hugging the mountain
When trucks barrel past—

If Satchmo. If Leadbelly—

If wind on the horizon,
Thundering the trees,
Making all of our houses small—

Notes

Some of the italicized lines in Part Four of "History" are drawn from the following sources:

The United States Constitution

"Six Weeks in the Sioux Tepees: A Narrative of Native Captivity," by Sarah Wakefield

William Apess' "Eulogy on King Philip"

"Man's Fulfillment in Order and Strife," by Robert Duncan

President Dwight D. Eisenhower's April 7, 1954 "Domino Theory" press conference.

The following italicized lines in "When Zappa Crashes My Family Reunion" are Zappa lyrics:

Great Googely Moogely!

Val-a-rie. Val-a-rie. Don't you want me? Don't you need me?

Ain't this boogey a mess? And knock the little jockeys off the rich people's lawns.

"Theft" is based on the October 17, 2003 *Chicago Reader* article entitled "Identity Theft" by Brendan Moore.

The title and some of the dialogue in "'Into the Moonless Night'" is drawn from the May 8, 2005 *New York Times Magazine* article, "Charlotte, Grace, Janet and Caroline Come Home" by Melanie Thernstrom, as well as "The Tale of Paraa," the central text of Alice Lakwena's Holy Spirit Movement.

TRACY K. SMITH is the author of *The Body's Question,* which won the 2002 Cave Canem Poetry Prize. She has received awards from the Rona Jaffe and Mrs. Giles Whiting foundations. She teaches in the Creative Writing Program at Princeton University and lives in Brooklyn, New York.

This book is made possible through a partnership with the College of Saint Benedict, and honors the legacy of S. Mariella Gable, a distinguished teacher at the College.

Previous titles in this series include:

Loverboy by Victoria Redel
The House on Eccles Road by Judith Kitchen
One Vacant Chair by Joe Coomer
The Weatherman by Clint McCown
Collected Poems by Jane Kenyon
Variations on the Theme of an African Dictatorship by Nuruddin Farah:
    Sweet and Sour Milk
    Sardines
    Close Sesame

The text of *Duende* is set in Adobe Jenson Pro, a typeface drawn by Robert Slimbach and based on late-fifteenth-century types by the printer Nicolas Jenson. Book design by Ann Sudmeier. Composition at Prism Publishing Center. Manufactured by Versa Press on acid-free paper.